More Praise for Crowns of Charlotte

"*Crowns of Charlotte* is sweet tea and something necessarily stronger, singing, ferocious—Lee Ann Brown's poems open forms and flora to an endless storm front. The reader finds herself (like the poet) a citizen inside, affixed to the generous field." —ELAINE BLEAKNEY

"Radiating an affection for true roots and veins of place, Lee Ann Brown expertly renders the crown in a name, and invites us to celebrate the 'School of the Imagination.' In *Crowns of Charlotte*, Brown is at her 'most vibratory' leading us to 'what happens through a new lens' where urban meets Appalachian, tradition meets revisionary embrace, and innovation collides with charmed reverberation. This is a book which unites worlds with great intelligence and beauty, and makes fluid the movement from child-mind to mother, lovingly weaving past and future into a stunning poetic sequence. Lee Ann Brown is a master of the constant 'now.' To read her work is to enter: flower, song, psalm." —LAYNIE BROWNE

"An autobiography 'of human DNA's complexity,' of the poet and the poem from inside their own helixes, of family and place from inside individual histories, and of the war culture from inside its radiant points of departure, *Crowns of Charlotte* offers 'multiple views of reality/in a single work' to demonstrate a thesis: 'every poem can be a new language.' Coiled within this thesis is the poet's perspective: 'We are the observer photographers of our personal ages/DNAs of each others' ways I am in the middle.' Working joyfully and elegiacally, sonically and visually, Lee Ann Brown creates poems that act as charged strands of DNA molecules 'in time to finger to find/The new way to unwind/Skeins of sound in mind.'" —AMY CATANZANO

"How rare it is, and how precious, that a poet with so many gifts decides to examine the terrain where she was formed, where her mongrel style was busy being born, one foot in the experimental cambium of her mind's poetry laboratory, and the other in the instinctive rhythms of balladry and folk songs, the myths and tall tales that inform her sensibility. Brown's lacework is a fine architecture, tough and tender at once, where she sits in the center of her quivering creations and spins like a sweet spider, giving us the language we need to tell the stories that are already within us, whose existence we had forgotten until now." —KEITH FLYNN

"Lee Ann Brown's ikebana sentences link material and maternal worlds to wreathe and doubly crown portraits of her home town with historical teeth marks. Take this auricular tour by a poet who knows what to do with skin texts we are too tight with. Here's a textural, textual matrix from a mother of invention." —JULIE PATTON

"Crowns is a 3-D spiral-ride, gravity pulling our body with the fortunes of a cast of characters of Brown's family (maybe-less-crazy-than-Flannery O'Connor's-citizens of-the-mind), and as the spiral we're riding widens out into the sky we let go like a weightless game of whip-the-tail, and we fly up from mountain peaks and for moments—like breaks in the clouds—we see everything at once." —REVEREND BILLY TALEN

Crowns of Charlotte

NC ODE

Lee Ann Brown

Poetry Series #15

CAROLINA WREN PRESS
Durham, North Carolina

Series Editor: Andrea Selch

Design: Lesley Landis Designs
Cover Image: "Marianna with Chandelier,"
        ©2006 Estate of Emma Bee Bernstein
Author Photograph: ©2013 Lee Ann Brown

The mission of Carolina Wren Press is to seek out, nurture and promote literary work by new and underrepresented writers, including women and people of color.

Carolina Wren Press is a 501(c)(3) non-profit organization supported in part by grants and generous individual donors. In addition we gratefully acknowledge the ongoing support of Carolina Wren Press's activities made possible through gifts to the Durham Arts Council's United Arts Fund. Special thanks to the North Carolina Arts Council for a grant supporting this publication.

Library of Congress Cataloging-in-Publication Data

Brown, Lee Ann.
[Poems. Selections]
Crowns of Charlotte / by Lee Ann Brown.
pages ; cm. -- (Poetry series ; #15)
Includes bibliographical references and index.
ISBN 978-0-932112-94-1 (alk. paper)
I. Title.

PS3552.R6932A6 2013
811'.6--dc23

2013015493

for my first family
MOM, DAD & BETH

TABLE OF CONTENTS

An autobiography that begins with one's birth
begins too late…
— Mary Lee Settle

I shall have a crown to wear when I get home
— Elizabeth Cotten

I started singing and they told me to stop
— Arcade Fire

How you praise the thing you're kind of unsure of…
— Kevin Young

You've got to go back to your roots
You've got to go back to your roots
You've got to go back to your roots…
— Cecil Taylor

(Radicality)

Rhizomatic

TRANSFORMATION HYMN

(to the tune of Ein feste Burg*)*

All mighty fortresses open your doors
All swords to ploughshares beaten

Why do our leaders lead us to war?
All vengeful hatred eaten

For still our ancient foe
Within us each doth grow

Our need this hour is great
Disarm this cruel fate

Our words of love undo it

MUSEUM OF THE ALPHABET

ACOUSTIC WINTER

If the year ends a plural spiral
Make it be so what a year is
If the winter begins again here
In the longest darkest place
Of the shortest bluest day
We play the stillness deep
Into the night song beside
All our sleeping family breath

Of the five friends I am holding
Who will last the winter
In their earthly spiral
In their spring trajectory
Move to lovely summer
One more lovely summer
Or further time to foil
Days whirl into nights

I move to see my parents
The ones who have born
Me out have borne me up
I move to be with my sister
And her local love her ones
I move to join the circle
I am already in my kith

Acoustic winter sings a summer
A way to stay awake as the light
Brings back its basket its halo
Its wreath of line and berries
Pine hurries to the wind again
Night is here at its most clear
Sound across the zones a weave
I sing this song again for winter

May Venus never sever
Her move across the sun
To come upon the next
Transit the next music
In time to finger to find
The new way to unwind
Skeins of sound in mind

AMONG US

We are each others
Mothers sisters brothers
Fathers once in camps
Or encamped behind wires

War is Over I thought forever
As I blew my cornet
In suburban back yard
Age twelve, 1975
Drew peace sign and dove

No way to recover
Someone so close to
Those close to me
Irrevocably gone
In Vietnam

Unthinkable to
Release us from one war
Only to tie us to another
And another
I had faith
In the world

World, world
Why are you still
Doing this killing?
How can seven thousand
Or is it over seventy thousand
Young Iraqi men be bulldozed alive
Under the burning sands of Iraq?

The war comes home
Why are people afraid
To open front doors
Children to roam around
We have to start again

A poet said to me
She was very tired
Yet went on to rest
Create again a place

To hold complex thought
Enmeshed in words
Race space place
For particolored people
New flavors raining
Down upon definition—
The Hmong among us become us

Tribal leaders ensconced
Story quilts of escape
Halfway to the mountains
Red cord and chicken foot
Around wrists
Seeds sewn into clothes

Khalor wouldn't go in the house
Our church gave her family
A bird (spirit) trapped inside
Battling windows with wings

No written language
Everything is alive
Sees the bondage around us daily
Next door slave times still crosstown

All children are our children
Growing up and living
All now our parents
Our work our word our world

APOCHRAPHAL

asphodel

that greeny flower

atop the rest-o-
rant

of restored ants

climbing through the bulletin's words

the wounds
by swords of cruel
centurions marked in jabs we hide

in *Le Balcon*

sister sifter memory

grown women now sit in the small place

now us

the mint passed down the row

Billy and Bobby before she and me

and who else are these knees bent to search the

free food of the year's yard

oniony stars of Bethlehem down the front walk

BALLAD OF WINSTON-SALEM

(to the tune of Pretty Peggy-O)

Sweet Deborah, she is dead, pretty baby, O
Sweet Deborah, she is dead, pretty daughter, O
Sweet Deborah she is dead
We lay flowers at her head
And across her final bed in the air-ee-o

The tabloids they are spread, Winston-Salem, O
The tabloids they are spread, Winston-Salem, O
The tabloids they are spread, they stain all our hands with red
No easy answers said, Winston-Salem O

The wrong man made to blame, O my listeners, O
There are daggers in the rain, O my listeners, O
The wrong one made to blame:
How can we untie their names?
And stop waking in the dark twenty years ago . . .

This act two lives entwine, everybody O
This act three lives entwine, everybody O
The one who's false accused, and the one who now pays dues
We sing their story now in this ballad, Oh

O sing and speak the news, O my poets O
O sing and speak the news, O my people now
The power of art is great, but can it stop the hate?
A woman still lies dead in the shadows Oh

Her mother's life's a hell, O my baby, O
Still spewing vitriol, O my baby, O
Somewhere further south, tears keep flowing from her mouth
A hunted man now freed, MAY HE LIVE IN PEACE

My babe, you're sleeping there, little daughter, O
I see you oh so clear little daughter, O
The veil of tears will grow,
How can I let you know?
How can I keep you safe in any air-ee-O?

Every time you see a flower, pretty daughter, O
Every time you see a flower, O my daughter, O
Every time you see a flower, think on its healing power
And cast it to the stream of the air-ee-o

BEFORE DAWN

*upon looking at Romare Bearden's mosaic of the same name
at the Charlotte Mecklenburg Public Library*

The door opens, backlit
On a round purple rag rug mimosa mosaic

Before Dawn opens the mosaic door
Backlit onto round rug rag in spiral

Broom propped near another mother watching
Her daughter carry a bowl of green, round

Figs or sprouts? Her grandmother beckons
Open palmed over patchwork tablecloth

Of orange ball & bluegreen squares. At the same
Moment my mind flickers to my mother

Taking care of my daughter. I am the woman
Shadowing the doorway watching them play

Watching thy / my mother

BEING THE LIKE

When his mama my sister asked her Nathan
What do you want to be for Halloween?

He answered
I want to be **Like**

      Like what?

Like a Diamond in the Sky

You want to be a Diamond
                    or a Star?

No, I want to be **Like**

      It has a black cheek
             a white cheek
    No ear   No eye
    No shoes
        On no feet
            No mouth

    & it has a **microphone**

BIRD / DREAM CONDUCTOR

Julie Patton is my conductor

She says

No wonder you're a poet
growing up around all these birds

Owls look down
on our last days at the house

Sleep with your window open
You need other people for this poem

Write down a line or two of images from your dreams
Commemorative vases smashed from Asian wars

Aunt Patty is so young in my dream
and has made an album of songs liturgical
She serves communion

I did smash something here—a moth

No mend piece
A post-traumatic era

Everyone get a bird noise
and start in soft and slow

Orchestrate it louder and all together

Then conduct an experiment in sound

Julie holds up DREAM sign

(Everyone tell your dream here)

Then bird noises in serial orchestration

     at random

        then

pointillist

She evolves a pattern of bringing people into the mix

a duet
then sections playing off each other
take the lead

then fall back

and play

One bird / One dream / One bird / One dream / Bird / Dream / Bird / Dream
(All)

CAR CONVERSATION

(Mom)

John Dudley wanted to write his big sister a letter
He couldn't keep a secret

So he wrote

Dear Dora Lee,

[blank page]

[blank page]

[blank page]

Then

We're moving to Norwood!

7th 8th 9th 10th grade went by

There were some girls who liked him

The first night he went to youth fellowship in Concord
he came home and said
I met a girl in a blue dress

We moved from Waxhaw in '48 when there was a polio ban
so we couldn't say goodbye to anybody or meet anybody new

I was sixteen so I wanted to learn to drive so
he took me out to practice in the L-shaped parking lot

I learned to back up better than go forward
That was a special time of him honing my techniques

I memorized that Driver's Ed book
Cover to cover
And all they asked me on the test was
Why do you dim your lights at night?
and
What is an eight-sided signpost?
My daddy took a new calling
It was still secret that we were going

I got to be valedictorian

Shift it low as possible

Helen Sanford, Terry Sanford's sister, was our English teacher
and beloved Miz McNeil

Made that cute brown quilt Dudley took to camp
She had a feeling that he was going to be born

And if you put Coca-Cola on top
of vanilla ice cream it's a flip flop

Air Force hospitals were not known for giving much anesthesia

When she was born she didn't even cry!
I took too big a whiff

Exactly 1:30, Bob
Keep that foot on the accelerator

Church sign by roadside:

If God is your Co-Pilot
Switch Seats

There were two Methodist churches in town:

One was singing
Will there be any stars in my Crown?
and the other, answered,
No, Not One.

The seniors taught the juniors how
to dance in the gym with records

I told them my mother & daddy
were very much in favor of me dancing,
I just didn't know how!

It was loud, rowdy dancing

I didn't know how to dance on the cruise

My partner said kindly,
Oh it must be the rocking of the ship
when I stepped on his foot

I could have clued him in
That just made the town go kerflop

A postcard of the main street
that was just all grass

       Church Marquee:
       America Bless God

A huge weight over the Amen Corner
Could have killed that whole family

After the sermon, our father, the preacher,
wondered why his whole car was covered with red dust outside
(Dudley and company had taken a joyride)

Well everybody knows everybody in a little town
Good and bad

Signs along the way back:

Stuffy's
Taxidermy
&
Game Processing

Keys
Gun Shop
Concealed Carrying Cases

Bait   Tackle   Ammo

Squirrel Level Road

No Grease
School of Tonsurial Arts

&

Elizabeth's
"Purdy"
Trucks

CHARLOTTE JARGON

basically, you have three choices:
jail, mall, museum —Jasper Bernes

Gucci-Teeter and Ghetto-Teeter
meet up nights on the Plaza

Taj McColl sways its way
through Uptown jukebox Overstreet Mall

The Overcash House, pink
The Diamond done over
The Coffee Cup done gone forever
where Charlotte met up for a trotter

I'm getting eaten alive
as I strive to write amidst all these skeeters

CHEERFUL RAIN

Plops up in round drops
Makes twenty day lilies appear

Today we find enough berries for pie
Poison ivy grows here too says Mom
So watch out where you pick

We put on heavy sweaters
Despite the heat
So chiggers
Won't get under our skin

Thin circlet of bites
Waist and wrist

We wade into overgrown fields
(All built up now)

Find blackberries heavy with dew
Purple blue-lobed plump and sweet

In the morning a musical shuttle
Runs between birds

Last night's rain has turned to mist

The woods are inhabited by singers
& drinkers of cheerful rain

CRISTO REDENTOR WAR SONNETS

for CA Conrad

Better late than never
Except when late means dead
on the grid of existence
Sighing the petition against war—
MLK spoke out against All Wars
As a pacifist he dismissed the fist
We're here amidst the unwrapped gifts
Day after Xmas and where are we
in terms of peace
Do it to the least of these my
Brethren & Sistren & you do it
Unto me—times three—Holy Trinity
    Calling all you who live in war—
    That state we do abhor

Fistula expatriated miss-ills
Cast down thy lot oh Cristo Redentor
Signs say pick it up & put it away
No joke—My now-gone uncle
was shot down in mid-flight transport
Plane—the family's still recovering
from "friendly fire" 50 years later the map
of Vietnam my grandmother tore down from her wall
Heartsick pins marked her baby
son's locale—who handed her
the second breath of spring
in a town so small the main street
    was grass—And how can I pass
    the fact his kids who were then 4 & 8

At the time of his death
Have none of their own?
My Iraqi family smiles at me
from a photograph under the tree
How can we know another's complexity?
By knowing our own.
Another's path connects
over the mountains with our own
All paths lead to home
Written notes in Snow or Rain
The Horn comes in across the Bronx
Where all our food & waste
    Flows in & out—the back room
    of the Provenance of Beauty's tune

A DIME FOR EVERY DAY IT DIDN'T RAIN

Every summer
in the week of
Montreat
Granddaddy Van
told his kids
they could have

a dime for every day it didn't rain
so my mom said the same to us

Across the years
none of us made much money
on that one

though once the rain waited until just after dark
and on the technicality that it was already night
Mom gave us our shiny prize

but both rain and dimes are changing over time

DIVE BOMB

I stop and save a box turtle
from the middle of
Republican Church Road

Then hit
a flash of bluebird
with my windshield
a few miles later

On the radio
Jon Stewart reports on the formation of the
"Congressional Softball League"
in which teams are paired such that
there is a good chance that each team could win at least once

So the Republicans form a splinter group, saying
These rules punish the strong and reward the weak

This fine June morning the deer my dad reports dead
at the side of the road is tended to by vultures

DOGWOOD DAY PARADE

We *were* going
vanilla ice cream instead

never got to see the Dogwood Princess
never saw her

flower flowers pinned to her dress
or maybe dressed completely in them from head to toe

atop an ice cream float
in giant woody dogwood blooms

the nail holes of Jesus's dire dried blood affixed to their four leafy petals
green and brown anthers in their middle headache

the green man her husband to be
but Janie sings *Jesus Loves the Little Children*

into the mic

as Mom's white Chevy pulls off into the wind

DORA LEE ADORED

Dora flowers. Adore a flower. Dora rose, lily etc.
fern hands leave love. —Julie Patton

Dora adores flora

   and me, her Lee.

She is my Door

       to this world

Mom's psalms sing all the others.

It's a puzzle why through Tuesday's snow

Clouds of alternative ending come down

to it

Wishing for spring, on today, March Third, Mom you emailed me:
Today my picture appeared on the front page of the Local Section
of The Charlotte Observer under the title, "Fifty Blooming Years."

I was wearing a plastic rain

hat because it was snowing.

In my hand I carried a strange assortment

of yellow mums, pussy willows and ferns. I had

only 15 minutes left to arrange my moribana

in the Ikebana booth before the deadline.

Fellow club members had been there

working for days. Why the

Observer photographer
took me is a puzzle since all my friends
could have been featured.
I've had fun reactions
on the phone and Internet.   Love, Dora Lee

Love Dora Lee I would love to go on a walk with you
somewhere down Queens Road looking for spring

Springing for the deadline
Working for days
Took me is a puzzle
I have to work out

Is there fate
Or is there predestination
Within an unknown set
or range of days

We are the observer photographers of our personal ages
DNAs of each others' ways I am in the middle

I've had fun reactions being with you
Looking forward to
more Joy
> *More Joy*

AN EARLY ARTS EDUCATION

Our assignment is to paint zoo animals
so I paint a big yellow lion
with a brown mane
and long eyelashes
It's shaping up rather nicely
right before my eyes
when my teacher comes over
she who wheels
the little jars
of premixed colors
into our classroom
for a rare hour of painting heaven

I watch in horror as she paints
a black iron manacle
around the forepaw of my lion
then
despite my protestations
row upon row
of interlocking X's
over the entire painting

That's the fence
She says

EASEDROPPING ON MYSELF

Storm front
Sudden
No service
It's a dangerous thing
Carolina by-products
Bakery feeds
Carolina Chocolate Drops
Gaddy's Goosepond gone
An impending storm
Little PeeDee River
Jesse Helms Hall of Fame
Cornelia worked for him
Monroe where they filmed
The Color Purple

A cauliflower suspended
In the middle of a frame
The housing of a candle
Complete with living flame

My house is not arranged like Gloria's
Yet in my mind my poems
All must have space and time and place
And halls of flowers grown
Interior design

In an office house of peach
Inspired me to arrange my shelves
So I could be out of reach
So as to make my own designs
A maximalist fringe
White halls hung with grids of lives still to be lived

Gloria says
It's a poor dog that can't hold up its own tail

That's right.
A native intelligence and beauty
Virginia Dare Book Club

A little face of a girl who is mine
Time passing time
Long leaf pine

My mom collects the giant cones
Pine needles to braid
I alternate between seeing past
and suffocating slow southern drive

Hamlet, east of Rockingham

Think about Coltrane making this trip ever west to Charlotte

The longest greyest two hours I ever felt

Dangerous to look for all these traces

Of things you won't be able to see

What plaque can play the impetus

Of *A Love Supreme*

Just as Cornelia collected *beach relics*

Always living shells

Now illegal to pick up even sand dollars

Pottery Barn sells identical replicas all in a row

If there is nostalgia for the past

Here I yearn for the natural world just out of reach

FACE JUG

I was originally made to warn kids off the corn liquor inside me
Then my grins started popping up in your friends' moms' dens

Eyes popping out and lips peeled back over
Crooked toothsome jagged snarls
I watch you
from in front of a Japanese screen of pine
I'll meet you
on the street corners of Lincolnton

I am colored blue, green, or most often tobacco-leaf spittle

FOR THE NONCE

King Kong Kitchee Kitchee Kimee-O

    On a Lee and Lonely

Alive alive-O

kicking & screaming from narrative

erotic energy maintaining

Person al   no one there

  Heigh ho

Blame it on the sun

        the sonnet

      the rain

  Nobody home

Ok

  bough & balance to me

Earliest memory

     on the stairs

  Heigh ho

a wicker basket   lifted up

    with me in it
If you love me

   Ta Toe
If you don't love me

   Ta Toe

but don't leave me on these
Tole Tole teps taking tole

&

O Wa Tai Goo Siam

O Wha Taigoo

   Siam

O What Aigoos Iam

O What ag Oose I am

O What A Goose I

   Am   —   this parlor game

co- con (structed) with

 tour of Duty

of

   John Dudley

       Ballad of John Dudley

Tragic Caribou Suspended

John
Oh
Hon
Nearly

Did
Undid
Does
Lashing
Ever back on
You

Will serve
I
Love
Every
You

My mother's Brother
affixed to a star
stop the magical thinking
there is no romance of war
any either way
plane in mid-Air
cracked & broken
Floating not Falling
So soon enacted

The Absence of the map
upon the world
   Obaa tore down
after following his progress
   now fallen
My parallel sister
   no silk parachute
   My mother's Dark-haired Daughter
   Ma cousine

                    co
soeur[[

        co sign
        if only

at 3 her dad-taken

        photo

            a whole in the

                fair family fabric

        Detective   Detective

        said school   so off he went?

Now   in   —   some form of

        recognized

Mechanical genius   —   Uncle

            to the stars   —

That photo in offices

        of every Caribou team

    to remind

A sign of need for more

        control of every amplitude

Japanese photographer now dead
   touched it   —   front page news

The plane is falling

   is SNAPped

has stopped

     & fallen

unspeakable

    Apogee

               Type to enter text

<u>Unspeakable</u>

Back to childhood

   to

    the

2nd break of sky

     the

    2nd breath of spring

Do I remember him
       yes
A sliding door   —   glass
      near Dodo's

           porch   —
                   in &   out
    then gone   —

then gone   —

    Need to connect

   with cousins

Need to *put on a show*

    a theatrical production

  A dog name   Heidi

A clothes line   )   my first encounter with a handknit sweater
(grey)

    a red & black plaid
                                   coat

   what really matters is

   handmade—

FOSSIL MEMORY

Going through my grandmother's things
I come across a huge grey fossil
A spiralized shell with smaller ghost shells
Embedded and nestled in an Indian basket

It slowly dawns that this is the very same fossil
I have a distinct and guilty memory for years
       of holding in my little hands
        at my Great Grandmother's
90th birthday party

and it breaking clean in two—
two halves of a sheared loaf of bread.

But here it sits   fully intact

      no seam   or imperfection

In my memory it was pale orange, glowing
but my mom swears there is no other fossil

Guilt ascends from me—

      feathers of regret

ether
      of

Reverse snow—

FOUND

I don't want to get it all together
      I thought I was on my last leg
So I wrote a letter
Telling him to remarry
and he just laughed

I got a good report
So the letter lies unopened
At the back of the mineral file

HAIR WREATH

Give me a lock of your hair
To remember you by

Before the photograph was invented
Hair grew in Human memory

Cut in the light of no moon
Grows faster than the names
In the bank box along with
One flaming diamond and
Whatever else radiates
Out from the sphere
Of the family no DNA
In hair—only at the root
Most hair wreaths
were in a horseshoe shape
But this our family's wreath is a Circle
Gently shedding in the frame
Even a grey poodle hair beloved
In the fame of names herein is trained
to rhyme and twine crocheted
to the next door porch swing
In summer or in wintry fear
If losing sped up any faster
Here are the names of unknown
Relatives—and here I insert the
Word which is Japanese
For the category of Ancestors
Passed out of immediate bodily
Or anecdotal memory yet
Present here nevertheless
Passed into a slightly higher
Sphere above our gears
Planetary and sidereal
My stars
here they are

HANDMADE IN AMERICA

my parents' hands
held my fingers on either side
as I "walked" up stairs

my mother's hands arrange the flowers
my father's hand clips out the news
and sends it to me in the mail

as intertextual braille
I learned from him

wiry hand left hand
writing at the bottom of the page

mom's lofty spirals
an earthly spiritual pair

in a child's face we
trace back the fibered scripts
the ancestors pass
through her form
one by one per hour
morphology's power
blink or you will
miss your grandmother
or great grand uncle's sire
shifting there
beneath her hair

HOMECOMING

Five different kinds of fried chicken
and only one or two from a chain

green beans from August gardens
biscuits potato salad yellow and white

depending on the recipe
at the end of the long table

in casserole dishes
lots of homemade desserts

with marshmallows melted on top
just like the sweet potatoes
with pineapple ring things

Good Success says my Mom

being raised firmly predestinational
she sees Luck
as vaguely pagan

Coincidentally my grandmother
a minister's wife
was kinda psychic

My mom used to call her up to ask
Where did I put my scissors?
and my grandmother, she knew where.

One day a woman she had not seen
for over a year came by unannounced.
Lucky for Obaa that something told her
only minutes before

to pull that ugly little footstool
the woman had given her
out of the closet.

Or maybe luck had nothing to do with it.

One day Mom was taking care of a 5-year-old grandson.
Getting him quieted down for bed
she stroked the washcloth Rabbit pillow
where he should put his head
and said
My mother made this pillow for *your* mother
and
he asked
What was *your* mother's name?
           Agnes
and what was *her* mother's name?
           Dodo for Dora Dunlop
And what was *her* mother's name?
           Ida

And as Mom left the room
it dawned on her
it was February 14th —
Ten years to the day
since she had said goodbye
to her mother
on this earthly plane

IKEBANA

Measure line material
Across the vase
She introduced me early

            Shin

     Soe
               Tai

            HEAVEN
     MAN
             EARTH

     but I wondered,

What about

          WOMAN?

Three elements, not two
     here make fertility

Moribana means "piling up flowers"

The "throw-in method"

       was my favorite

originated by a samurai
     in a hurry

spearing purple iris

                    with his sword
always an odd number

                    off center

random chance
                    emulating nature

JUVENALIA

Spending the Night at Obaa's
            (Grandmother)

Pried from stories and food and books
    Mouth made minty
    ~~Face splashed~~
Face Washing Water—

                    High Bed
                Crisp Sheets
                    Sounds of Crickets
                Attic Fan
                        and Morning

LATERAL WING

word collage for Romare Bearden

Hook nose & belly
   in Aeolian mode

Multiple views of reality
   in a single work

Paul Valery said
Man's patience was destroyed by machine

I find collage a direct statement

We are all wedded to our...

Modern consciousness is a

   Composite

Composed of singular visuals

         Living on The Block
         Sees behind his façade

O moon over Edgecombe!

Uptown
looking Downtown

         One Charlotte Observer
                  of those stairs to nowhere

And rewriting

                    the
Shadow Side
                    (Slow Show)

Of course it's not easy
I know now as a mother
A something that goes a
Little wrong would magnify
In an instant
    or
over time
            you stay up later & later
or don't learn how to
                        swim
or drink the wrong things
            or never stop nursing
or all kinds of worries
            like will I remember
my own restlessness
            enough late night
to write them down
            separate from you

who equates
        I'm getting named
with loving

A LIST OF 19 SUITORS

So elegant my grandmother
So close to her father

That someone recognized her
A thousand miles away

Aquiline nose, large eyes
Skin translucent in photos

I knew her in wrinkles
Where I must have gotten
My under-eye designs

She had very fetching hats and
A sense of style to beat the band

When she brought the preacher
A cold glass of water

Clear eyes flash
Green goblet of glass

O perfect Love
He wasn't on the list

LOX ON GRITS

Being the ever-sophisticated New York City dwelling granddaughter I am, I brought my grandmother some delicacies from my favorite delicatessen, Russ & Daughters. The bagels proved too hard for Obaa's dentures, so Mom, always the improviser, plopped the lox on top of yellow grits usually adorned with butter and cheese hidden in the bottom of the bowl so they'd melt. I ate there at that table with them both and had visions of revolutionizing the East Village brunch scene, perhaps opening a Grits Booth next to the Live Juice stand on First and First where the bands hang out in the daytime. I could serve a wasabi cream cheese special. A syncretic invention: Lox on Grits.

MECKLENBURG EVENING

Catches the land and its trees
in that saturated light
before twilight
when the sun is angled into its most vibratory

No figures in the space
to suggest a temporary human condition
No space is inactive

The tangle of vines is suggested
This is no moss-covered south

yet deep enough to have many bees
The fall is bright and warm

The foothills rise from this piedmont
to the mountains   to the west

It's unbearable in summer sometimes
but not as hot as Faulkner's dark porch

I realize what ties us all
and animals too which we are

is the land

The history of what we have done to each other on it
complicates things

But everyone appreciates their own back yard gardens
and secret caves carved out from inside the bushes

MOMMY LOOK

(my daughter points)

Your favorite words!

                    STOP
                    WAR

MOM'S PSALMS

or

How to Rewrite the Bible

If King David could do it, so can we.

MUSEUM OF THE ALPHABET

You can't go home again but you can come here
says the School of the Imagination
to this hometown ode radiating out across the Piedmont

You can't swim in the same lake twice
especially if it's man-made
Lake Wiley or Norman which contains Garfish Cove

Wiley was one possible boy's name for our daughter
I was to be Van which rhymes with Ann
Why all this fascination with names?
Every word is made of letters
It's something to hold onto
however slippery

Include Everything in Poetry
even though
Everything Changes

The alphabet museum is an open form

Museum + Alphabet
two generative words
not often seen side by side

the poem as museum of the alphabet
with ever changing displays
according to who's walking through

If a language can be defined
as a vocabulary plus a set of rules
then every poem can be a new language

To revisit childhood scenes

is what happens through a new lens

We are not here to describe
say two young poets in conversation

I say
We are not here *only* to describe
but to revisit description in such a sway as to not close it down

Hang the coattail of the idea on the goldenrod

I come not to bury but to praise

NUMBERS

Of houses speed by
in the June ninth night
Misunderstood Venus transit
Nothing beats
drifting past houses
I used to live in
kindergarten buildings
in a church down the street I used to
go to every day
over a cement slab bridge
The French say it well
as a poetics of space
If the corner of a playhouse
is still there
and the cul-de-sac cat's paw
opens to a church of the open door unlocked

ODE TO ROMIE

        Collage takes the stripe
of sun & shadow rhythm
          from above
              the elevated train

      NC to NYC

Harlem is its own
      borough

Her hands

All is not even

  the emotion to let go

the Feel of the line

      in one's hand

  Repo Man—

    take back what the others haven't

      earned

recombine with birds

    the weeds of Queens

   goldenrod

     pastoral

in the vacant lot

the rhythm of the track

   overhead
the characters

         people on the block

   to sustain a note

      cut-up

         organic

   the movement of the

                  leaves

      Beauty supply

         It's a sign

   words

            eyes

   New platform

Amazing Hair ablaze

ODE TO UNCLE BILLY

Over and Out
Telegraph to Telstar:

The tramp of time
on the MacNeil-Lehrer hour

Word has it you cured me of a crying fit
by blowing a mote of dust in the sunlight
so my parents could have a little time to walk in a castle

Blowing Rock lifts up its leaves on the updraft
A source of early memory
Staying up very late in Spain or
tasting first strawberries and asparagus in Aranjuez

Smocked dresses you brought
every airport Easter aloft
in pastel egg colors
unveiled for me and my sister
Our mother keeps them in the closet
ready for daughters in stair-step sizes to come

Years ago my Miranda rode your foot like a horse
You looked at each other in wide surprise, eyes open

Mom caught the moment in a photograph

Like the one of me riding on your back
in this selfsame living room

on Beverly Drive
one of your childhood homes

where before, I remember your father
in wing chair

and similar brow
where your brother, my father, still abides

Uncle / grandfather
Billy and Bobby

linked in intricate bonds
Analogous pair
as only brothers can be

Words like Unduraga and Rioja
rolled from your tongue
during nuestra comida

You took me on a foray to Harris Teeter
for fresh grapes
to rescue the fillets of sole Véronique
from being polluted by Mom
who fished grapes from a can of fruit cocktail

All that old-time on the radio
sounded like *Briarhopper* music—
You waited till late-night airwaves
brought in the classical waves

Wagner's just a lotta noise
You prefer Verdi
and choice cuts of string quartets

Rarified cufflink stacks
of the centuries' best news

you repeated to me:
Write it up!
Like fine wine, a communion

to pour, recur, recite, renew
in future memory reverb, Fugue
Variations on a life

Irreducible, a true original
A human music

ONCE REMOVED

ask that flowers be omitted

  the bride wore

    three quarter sleeves of my mother's dress once removed

      so my arms could fit inside

        married ten years later than my mother

  not as delicate

and she married ten years later than hers

  thus accordioning the generations apart

a parallel family to ours reproduced more efficiently

      thus fit four generations of friendship

interlocked with three of ours

our granddaddies, both preachers

as a joke   sent a brick back and forth

  "Collect on Delivery"

to signify a new baby born

  their family received more bricks than ours

 was it the same brick or a pile of bricks?

 this part of the south seems to be made of brick

pink taffeta rose

and finally nothing

the new south slowly eating the old

a purple area of the state   very blue   and very red

   like in the mountains of Madison now

      very very white   heard tell of a history of bad signs on the roads

   and Bible verses too

         painted on a rock

      is it always the same verse?

I about had a wreck   trying to photograph

      a hand-painted placard on a truck in front of me
when the migrant referendum was up last summer

here in Charlotte the two sides of town
      seemed so demarcated   there are roads I've still never traveled
when I worked downtown
               which we're supposed to call Uptown
         I caught the bus on the "wrong" side of the street
and my Daddy had to come pick me up
               on the way back to the depot
      because the bus service stopped at seven

      but I digress
   I started out talking about what the bride wore

and started thinking about geography and driving
   and the radio interview on Fresh Air

where Chris Rock
talked about how his stand-up comedy skills
were related to his granddaddy's preaching
and all the tricks he saw up his sleeve

my mom was a Preacher's Kid
        who didn't really rebel
so I felt I had to doubly do it

I grew up with a Daddy whose family
        went to the same church for six generations
The First Church gathering out under the trees
        near the crossroads of Trade & Tryon

a long line of preachers with Scottish muttonchops
        photos on the wall of the narthex
a hidden wooden panel in the back of a closet
        leading to a secret tunnel to the underground railroad
a tall steeple we used to dare each other to climb up in
        across Z-shaped ladders

mostly we sat in the balcony
        and drew our own tunnels
between the words on the bulletin
absorbing years of litany
in a certain order
in the eye of the storm
        and standing
with my family
to sing the hymns

        but I digress

ONE WHO OWNS A CROWN

A baby's head is said to crown out of a mother's own womb — up South, down North — I turned my mouth quickly to mom's nipple against my cheek in the dark of the Chapel Hill planetarium. I'll crown you over how to pronounce bad with one syllable or two. My maternal lion Lee in all her permutations—five Agnes Lees back to Scotland — only one I ever knew consciously in life. Miranda's name contains Reality as well as Annie Lee as I gather my father's mother was named though I never met her. Agnes Lee Wiley saved up the pages of her address book and presented them to me one Christmas Eve generously reminding me I was on the move a restless spirit like thee who reads or listens thus far to this aisle of text—this text I'll weave a crown of hair of others who share a tress. The word of the day is Affinity—Tokyo has the same latitude as Charlotte so the cherry trees blossom at the same time.

THE ONLY GUN I WOULD WANT

Aunt Virginia shot skeet
with Uncle Wilbur
Agnes Lee saw Annie Oakley ride
Even though she's allergic to it
Mom showed me how to
pick a stem of English plantain
bend it over on itself to form a loop
so the top can slide in and out
and then
pull it through fast enough
to POP the top off
and hopefully hit something
with the fuzzy green bud

PERSIMMONS

This evening
    my mother took my father
        out into the dark to pick
    persimmons she found on a
walk before dusk

No one else knows they are there

  except her
now he

and I now

am in a pear, a roll of the dice
is nice   that's the way I like it

To return to a pattern variation
    always interested
        a familiar   never the same

Bright the sky—then cold
  grey black—the way I
    itch for love or something

My daughter wakes me
    in the middle of the world
        dark night—where's summer?

I can't even
make a decision
in the daily life sometimes

The wind blows
The weather soars

I can't get warm
    sometimes unless
he's there

Finally time
    to turn on the
boiler, the water

That's what I am

doing is making
together and apart
a life is spinning
a thread this way

and the other way
    then both together
a strengthening in doubling
    turning in opposite ways
in-vined
    soluble as water
the very fabric of cells does that

    We eat the permissions
together remember again

what's important the groundswell
    the waves we catch and are in
the sand beneath pulling away to new platforms

As the crow flies
        and
            as the dog walks on

we glimpse cold mountain
as we still speed past

RIC FLAIR

I never saw much wrestling as a child
but I did watch me some Roll-R-Derby

Immobile after all those
Saturday morning cartoons were over

And I did play some mean Roll-R-Bat

But I knew it was a special day
When Ric Flair himself

Walked into Scarlet O'Hair's
Holding a gold suitcase

His platinum shag needed some doing—
A flag from some other kind of world

I had yet to see

ROGUE ROBOCALLS FROM HAITI

land in the fields of Fayetteville
and people heard "bomb" in a foreign tongue

which was most likely "bonne"
praising a politician
running for election

so they ran for their lives
and evacuated the whole town

You can see the constellations from anywhere on earth
but only the comets land here

SAMPLER (LO-FI)

a child is   and everyone   is
constantly scanning the horizon

for affection

Dub Atomic Particles
good driving music

in the south the lanes are bigger   less cars

can you turn it down a touch please
the big fight scenes I can't take

I come across a happening
   on the drawbridge
of a school

she is moving with strings attached
   elasticity   suspends her
as it restricts her movements   she deliberately slows

the child is close   curious
inserting herself into the scene
   bold and no one stops her

participatory   as we are who watch
   incomplete   I come upon it

watch for a stranger to soon become a friend

brrreathless
to encounter interested parties

the air is kicked up a notch
   a quality of attention

when you take time to paint on the windows

and give yourself permission to rewrite the songs

and sample   and mix

it up

she   is moving through space

fix   black   before   and   in

how lyrics embed themselves

their particularity

that weird "personal" to "universal" effect

as a mother I know about constantly checking in
the back and forth communication

the pull of the outside world

on a child   is strong

I felt it myself
very young

maybe one of my first memories
walking up a path behind my parents

the foggy day has lifted
white that enveloped the playground

has dissipated
and we are walking up an incline   a dirt path

to the right

my parents are together

I hear bird noises
to my left

emanating from a little shed
coo coo coo

are they trapped or do they live there

I want to see the birds
that make such beautiful noises
but
they are   mysterious
behind a wooden door

in a narrow shed

I am being called away
   to the gravitational pull of my parents

that effective way I know now
  when the child will not come along

to move deliberately away
and they do
come

that pull   is strong
I stretch the bond

my life started in search of bird noises
I want time to open that door   now

and more doors
give my child that time   that permission

have you felt the incredible empathy
children have for animals

because they know they *are* one
coming into language

on the edge of language
and the way children sound like birds
before sentences roll out unimpeded

permutational whirrs and coos
colors of musical variation and elation

being in that flow   of words coming into being

spoken from a mouth   sung from a small mouth
across from you   a mouth you helped to make

now speaking her own ways

I went back twenty years later
to that landscape
opened up

arbor-covered hillsides

a proliferation of tiny garden sheds
the multiplicity of it all

how much further I could see

sometimes I return to that hilllside
to wonder at the many hidden things
the tiny handmade buildings
amongst the vines

each plot tended   towards a larger cultivation

in dream   in poetry

open them carefully
to talk with the birds
reject the closure of the doors

'SCUSE MY BOARDINGHOUSE REACH

Having lunch by myself
at East Boulevard restaurant
which used to be a bedsit where
Carson McCullers lived in one room in the back
with her young husband,
and my great-grandmother
ran a boardinghouse next door
in the house with the turret which is now a law office which
I always thought was her house but in actuality she rented
and then in turn sublet to the all the people she also fed

So there I was eavesdropping as usual and
these three ladies were encountering the lunch menu
and one said:

Mabel, I think I'm gonna try some of this here Quee-chee

SHORT TALK ON MS WORD

When I was twelve years old I got my mom to buy me this curvy navy blue T-shirt with the word "Ms." inscribed in white type across my chest. I was also attracted to a T-shirt that was emblazoned with an image of a Mae West type perched on a florally bedecked bicycle with her bosom thrust out in front, side view, like the prow of a ship. This was at the Gap where the other essential piece of the conform-i-form uniform was purchased: Levi's thin-gauge cords in powder blue or burgundy. Even though old-fashioned, the photographic T-shirt was deemed too suggestive for purchase with its visual representation of bosoms, but the empowering new word "Ms." with its big impending period was sexy enough for me and became an emblematic garment for a while. I was becoming my own Microsoft Word: "MS Word" to you.

SLAW

(typed on Mom's Presbytery Stationery)

I take showers
until the new idea comes
or the hot water runs out whichever comes first

My grandmother is going in & out of time
and sleeps she says without any dreams

Looking out the backseat window, being driven by Dad
I see the red clay's "ring around the collar"

washed up on the split-level house's bricks
before shrubs are put in to hide the stain

Now I have to go put the finishing touches on dinner
before they miss me and say I've shirked my sisterly duties

SOME OF THIS EVENING'S THOUGHTS DURING A NORA JANE STRUTHERS CONCERT

in memorium Tina Parker

My cousin Malcolm just said he loved me on the phone

flashback to when I was four or so and we were
drinking Cheerwine, the soft drink of the Carolinas
I got the cap off and looked down into the bottle
before tasting that fizzy cherry cola in Freedom Park

Mac said *I am SO Hot*
I think I am going to take off my shirt

and five-year-old me said *Me too!*
and eight-year-old cousin he said *NO DON'T!*

I honestly wondered why he was getting so upset
and when I realized it was cuz I was a girl
I got mad about gender equality even then

Years later I *dove* into the mudhole off the bank
in order to do one better than the boys who just jumped
That's why I always crick my neck like I do now

I treaded water for an hour
under the lifeguard's tower
Asked him to time me
so I could double some boy's thirty minutes

Growing up was hard
around beautiful creatures like Tina Parker
I used to write down her outfits

The one time I went over to her house
I saw her older sisters' nail polish rack

They did a dance routine at Dana Auditorium
to a song called "Steam Heat"

Imagine my embarrassment
when she detected unseen buds
under my dark green bodysuit
ribbed polyester with snaps
and Tina Parker told me to GET A BRA

I told my mom what she said
and she took me straight to Belk's
In the dressing room
I wanted to back out of the whole proposition
but Mom said *No, it's too late now*

When coming into my own
I worked one summer at the Public Library
Hanging out in the break room with older women, they'd say
"Lee Ann, did you have any *childhood memories* this weekend?"
after I told them I had childhood memories
whenever I made out with someone

Keep the Queen City the Clean City
is what was written on all the trashcans of my childhood
and there was a Rugby team called The Charlotte Harlots

Escape the preppie tyranny of the add-a-bead

Charlotte was *almost Nashville.*
And they all go naked on a Saturday night

You can't buy happiness you know says Nora Jane
"Yeah but you can rent it" a low voice from the audience replies

The only time I was aware of the Summer of Love
was when Romper Room's Miss Debbie

turned the year 1968 to 1969 on the sticky felt wall calendar on TV
My parents told me Romper Room came from the little building
behind the great glass mountain but years later I realized
they meant the tower behind the Coliseum
was beaming it in from someplace else

Then it was 70s Charlotte
where highlights of our modern culture
were visits to the Intimate Bookshop at Southpark Mall
and getting a 45 at The Record Bar near the Chick-fil-A

Fashion was once a year fake Tretorns from Woolworths

the parking lot of Ovens Auditorium where Dad had to safety pin
my green bowed vintage disintegrating dress
cuz I was busting out all over on the way to Jamie's graduation
close as butter on toast

Tina Parker, the last time I saw you
was on the news
in a hotel room in Hickory
during the first Obama debates
You were in a red convertible
getting interviewed for cutting into the long line for gas
and I always thought I'd see you again

SYBIL NOIR

for Melanie Neilson

Strange gossip coincidence
small town sneaky blather

Ladies in violet sweaters
        with pearl buttons
sing "Bye Bye Love" starting at the 'xact same neuron impulse
and then key change up to the Batter Hymn of the Mighty Sparrow

One saliva bubble Chickamauga
tintypes of strewn body parts
in the new miracle of photography—

Raft of the Medusa
spits on Huck Finn's
narrator fixing to
recount his no 'count account
of the ways of all flesh
engaging with the Other (which is the text)

At first it's lowercase obscure difficulty
then becomes alive, drives it home

THOMAS WOLFE WAS SO TALL

he put his typewriter
on top of the refrigerator
in the old Kentucky Home

My Aunt Cornelia
upon hearing that Mr. Wolfe
was dining at the President's home
at Chapel Hill 1937
rushed over with her Brownie camera
which didn't have a flash
so he obliged her and went into the yard
to have their portrait taken together
under the pines

I wonder which voluptuary sentences
ran through her mind
to make her want to seek him out so
but I can still talk with her about it
seventy years later
down the road in Cary
in her room of "beach relics"
which is what she calls shells

I can lift the phone to my ear
like a conch back in time and take note

I went to to the Dean's house to meet him
I was so entranced at his use of words

and he could express himself so well

Oh wouldn't that be heavenly!
to use the English Language that way

They had him already scheduled to lecture at several different classes
English   History

Well anyway when I got there he was eating

      but I remember I lost the others
      at some point

      what could I do

When I would lose the crowd
I would dive over backwards

they escorted me back to the group
a misstep and I went overboard

well this is the last I'll see of that group of boys

draft the men into the army
and they would be in the lower group

keep me down the road straight

(My husband) died the same week Stuart was born

collapsed on shipboard
officers were designated to walk around the ship
12-hr duty   they had to be alert because of submarines

the name of the ship
similar to Look Homeward Angel

pneumonia   diagnosed it as malaria

day before he died he was in a hospital in New York City

they were mighty slow in letting me know

your husband is seriously ill
same day: Your husband's condition has changed to critical
very critical

next day   talked to whoever would answer
they took forever to answer

well tell me about what he has I said
what's the forecast for people that have malaria

viral pneumonia   they didn't have penicillin
he died within 2 days within 2 days after that

We would walk the coastline
I would immediately start picking up shells

I tried my best to get Stuart interested in shells
I failed

various places in Florida
they are manufacturing artificial shells

but if you look at them carefully they are all alike

whole shoeboxes full of sand dollars
that's distressing to me

sitting on the porch
I had a course in geometry

333-2451 SUSIE ASADO BREAKDOWN

+

Sweet Tea

Sweet, sweet Susie is a sure
          on this.
Slips the clean it.
It silver is please, please to jelly.
The say to a Incy.
A pot is a bit if trees, old bobbles
          which shove clean.
Must pups.
Pups see it, a pins, a what.
A unison.
Sweet, sweet tea.

+

What I really wanted to say is:

      Sweetened Ice Tea with lemon & mint on the back porch of
333-2451 on a glass table top. Susie Worthen next door sunbathing,
her mother's silver left unpolished on the porch. Pot is a bark of musty
puppy & a pin, sewing & singing in unison.

+

	tea
	&
	the porch—
(sunbathing)	(a next
	door
	mother's
	polished
	porch)
	musty
	&
	singing

WAXHAW

When they first arrived Agnes saw a little pig
running down the street and wondered where she'd landed

They were paid $100 a month by each church
plus a once yearly "pounding" at Christmas

A pound of flour here   a pound of sugar there
some chickens to live in the yard

the floorboards were so far apart
the wind came up making the rug
float up like a flying carpet

my mom ran from the tub to warm herself
by the hot potbelly stove
got too near once and
her bare little bumpty bore
"zebra stripes"

eavesdropping through a vent in the ceiling
she could hear her Daddy counsel couples to be wed

when the women of the church had a luncheon
everybody at the long table had a little glass of sherry
but they didn't give any to Agnes—no not the preacher's wife

When Van accepted the call to the next church
Agnes cried into a big bowl hand-painted with flowers

WINGHAVEN

First the Archway

and through the gate
past Ligustrum amurense
and the burfidi holly and
that's just prickly old Mahonia
Elizabeth Clarkson didn't really like
so she stuck it in behind the garage but
the birds loved it and scattered it all over
so she said   *if the birds like it so do I*
this garden made of a slippery red clay lot
and years and years of anniversary and birthday
presents of brick brick brick for walkways and walls
a lush formal garden for the birds complete with poetry

The Laughing Bench

The lines are fallen
unto me in pleasant
places: Yea, I have a
goodly heritage.
                —Psalm 16:6

An impossibly hot walking town in August
yet I insist on exercising my familiar ones

The sidewalks unroll like we're underwater
and the leaves fall even at the height of summer

It's hard to fake writing about something if I'm
not in it   but it is possible   Everyone tries
to put birdsong into words   but it's not right
like that one who just sounded like a musical

shuttle or tiny hurdy-gurdy not *Tea Kettle*
or *Hey Sweetie*   3 glass ashtrays still on

the windowsill full of birdsong, mealy worms
no less a banquet left on the bench beside me

gathered from discarded country club crape
myrtle clippings after the rainstorm that

produced three fireballs down the line in August
we were without power in the old Park

gradually turning itself over to the new South
yet replete with lovely overgrown back alleys

and all the sweetgum balls you could want
to collect my mom taught me never to pass

up something free that could be made into
another thing   Hands on hips, mom quotes Kagawa:

Though my muscles may stiffen,
though my skin may wrinkle,
may I never find myself yawning at life.

here we are
through the sighline

touching the softest boxwoods
imaginable who lap at
my hand like a pet

white wrought iron on
the way to our hideyhole
and a whistle in the distance
I want to be ever a child

this is the domain of the birds
i have an idea

you and me are going to sneak
very quietly past the feeding box

where'd you get those tadpoles?
We ask the gardener
I got them at lunch
He replies

      …. the raindrops,
the flowers, the insects, the snowflakes.
I want to be keenly interested in everything,
with mind and muscle ever alert, forgetting
my troubles in the next moment.
The stars and the seas, the ponds and the trees, the birds
and the animals are my comrades.

Pear tree so tall!
like the one in our backyard
when we were small

you gave our pears
a little rolling kick
to rid them of bees
before you picked them up

let nothing trouble thee,
let nothing afright thee

...a varnish tree...

within the seed a tree,
within the glowing egg a bird

       canopy of leaves
a green tunnel
2 cardinals traverse the path

   For unto whomsoever much is given
of him shall be much required:

           I cast out a new sort of boat

beyond the circular pond

nor doubt our inmost wants are known

therefore, be still

     no body knows where we are

YELLOW CANARY CAFE

To eat To eat
in neon

When you can study
what you like
you can go to town

Why study history?
Like Foucault for me
It's in the daily details

That Agnes Lee
thought "SS" deducted
from her paycheck

Meant "Sunday School"
rather than Social Security
or something darker
Shows the centrality

Of church to her life
as social milieu, governance
and livelihood

Lengthening of dresses
yard work, menus
and things of beauty

Noted haiku-like
Maple tree
Make her live for me

In her Line-a-Day Diary
Where huge gaps
of days point to
the vast business of
caring for one then two

Babies or the book
misplaced or
perhaps a vast sorrow

Unable to be expressed
in words

DOUBLE CROWN FOR CHARLOTTE

for Cecil Giscombe
who first told me my hometown's namesake,
Queen Charlotte of Mecklenburg, had some African ancestry

"The portraiture will hide her African features, but history will not."
—Tisa Bryant, *Unexplained Presence*

1.

The town I grew up in is feminine
a radiating spiral divided in two
named for Charlotte of Mecklenburg, a Queen
who had mixed bloodlines all of them blue:

African, Portuguese and a Vandal or two.
So this double crown I set out to hone—
half on, half off, made-up and true.
Fifteen sonnets linked and sewn

in all manner of newfangled rhyme;
only locals know which avenue
wends over to trace a parallel line.
Crowns for Charlotte, Laurels for you—

Queen Charlotte of Mecklenburg now come forth
to crown us all with a laurel wreath—

2.

To crown us all with a laurel wreath—
we filed in with our teacher one by one
from a yellow school bus, young and green
to find words worn by others as well as our own.

I remember standing before her portrait alone,
a golden palanquin completing the scene.
Larger than life, next to her throne
Charlotte stood, suspended, draped and lean.

Tapered blue shadows cast on a column—
"White House"—purple Hellenic—uncurled
on black fur dots in soft white ermine
to her sleeve, a lacy cauliflower unfurled

Choker high up—pearls loop—show her worth
I saw a map early on of North and South

3.

I saw a map early on of North and South
Carolina combined,
labeled Carolus & Caroline
drawn from the jagged coast
left to the west
to no end line
just one long swath
<—THAT way
Hell to the other
side of the planet
not even
drawn
& quartered yet
a gloss written in between lines

4.

A gloss written in between lines
of this poem penned for her wedding day:

Descended from the warlike Vandal race,
(The Vandals were Germanic, did vandalize)

She still preserves that title in her face.
(Her face her face now that's the trace)

Tho' shone their triumphs o'er Numidia's plain,
(Numibia—now that's surely Africa)

And Alusian fields their name retain;
(All the family's here!)

They but subdued the southern world with arms,
She conquers still with her triumphant charms,

O! born for rule, to whose victorious brow
The greatest monarch of the north must bow.

5.

The greatest monarch of the north must bow.
But who's that for us now?
Complex corporate fools or rules?
Having to work as others' tools?
Let's consult the *Children's Miscellany*
under the crazy monarchs entry:
"One king, fearing he was made of glass,
stuck iron rods down his clothes—another's
favorite pastime was to wedge himself
into a wastepaper basket and roll
around on the floor. And a Belgian queen
had such a severe phobia of fleas
she had a tiny cannon to fire
in the bedroom." King George whines

6.

In the bedroom. King George whines:
I've had no peace of mind
Since we lost America
Forests old as the world itself
Meadows, plains
strange delicate flowers...
Immense solitudes

and all Nature new to Art
All Ours
Mine
Gone
A paradise
lost, and Charlotte says
O sing

7.

O sing
for my little dog Presto   O sing
for my fifth daughter's white nightdress   O sing
for my husband's shaving brush & mug   O
sing for the partition of linen that
swings in the evening air beside my bed
that shelters me from ever watchful eyes
When I pull out my little pack of notes
O sing for my India ink & my
little wooden lap desk where I can stake
my claim yet again *O sing for that which*
is ordinary goes down to Orcus
unsung this ordinary song   O sing
of human DNA's complexity

8.

Of human DNA's complexity
King George Three perhaps had porphyria
which made him mistake a large tree
for the King of Prussia (plus he had blue & purple pee)

Listen to this: One note from 1811 reads
His Majesty's medicine was given
him by force at seven o'clock and this
has certainly contributed to his irritation

and irascibility which has prevailed ever since...
Arsenic in that dose made him worse
and Charlotte had to cope while he lost it
and the Colonies big time, of which she

wrote, they *make me always compare them to*
a dog which shows its teeth but never dares

9.

a dog which shows its teeth but never dares
to bite such a difficult place as history
This is how a poem can breathe,
tear itself open to epiphany

The Vertical Files and Ephemera
Collection are often ignored
but here's what I found and pulled out for you:
It takes ten seconds to make a baby

and that could be anybody says the librarian—
Family trees can be a tricky thing to climb...
She reads off a long list of 60s riots
to someone on the phone as *Lady Sarah, dressed*

as a shepherdess makes hay by the road
To decode a painting one has to get close

10.

To decode a painting one has to get close
and see a letter in Charlotte's own hand
beside three other portraits all very different
as if the court depicters had a hard time

making her "look good" and also like Herself.
Sir Allan Ramsay's portrait showed Charlotte's
true mulatto face and traveled all over the place,
so the royal pair could tower over their subjects.

Before the split from Mother England, Charlotte called it
Eine kleine Erschütterung (a little shake-up) but nothing decisive.
Later: *This diabolical war will continue to cost a lot of blood.*
Cursed be those who encourage the rebels.

There were loyalist women
Who didn't want to let go of their Queen

11.

Who didn't want to let go of their Queen?
Women made in tribute a quilt pattern:
Queen Charlotte's Crown
in geometric symmetry flaming.

Of those who come to the portraits,
some come away disappointed
when they find Charlotte isn't more "African of face."
The copper sculptures show her green.

Gainsborough painted Phoebe and Mercury,
her Pomeranians, to each look like lions.
We are all of us multicultural
even the Queen of England.

Compass of her voice: *Genius of Music at her side:*
Sophia Charlotte was also a painter.

12.

Sophia Charlotte was also a painter
as we know from letters to her brother
asking him to buy anonymous supplies
before the color is applied or after...

ask discretely whether they use white in the color
& by which means do they achieve
their nuances. Charlotte was a pacifist
which attracted King George in the first place.

Who will take such a little princess as me?
A proposal from across the sea.
She practiced English hymns
while her ladies-in-waiting were seasick over the side.

One portrait shows her hair caught up in a kerchief
But my favorite is a photograph.

13.

But my favorite is a photograph
of my mother and daughter in front of
her off-center sculpture at the airport
on one of our many arrivals in town.

My daughter wears a homemade crown.
Charlotte holds out her diadem in the wind
in the distance for all of us to wear.
Her curvilinear form dances to vectors

of NC jet stream—an old southern town
now on the pathways of the world in
a different way than when it was a
Trade road of Cherokee to Uwharrie

or when George Washington slept here.
Do me the favor to burn this if you love me and believe me.

14.

Do me the favor to burn this if you love me and believe me
in baroque Domesticity—six children—one a baby
on her lap—nine yet to come and two
to die beloved here all beribboned

and shining blue royalty—she the true
Ruler—Zophany shows her in the family
way—a clear gaze I hear Charlotte's
plain song now—I am one Charlotte Observer

Still piecing the puzzle together
in an open way, conversing with space
Bodies or bodices, sutures in the light—
Who are you in this living duet?

My answer is coming yet
Adieu. All yours   Charlotte

15.

The town I grew up in is feminine—
To crown us all with a laurel wreath
I saw a map early on of North and South.
A gloss written in between lines:

The greatest monarch of the north must bow
in the bedroom. King George whines:
   O sing
of human DNA's complexity—

A dog which shows its teeth but never dares
to decode a painting. One has to get close.
Who didn't want to let go of their Queen?
Sophia Charlotte was also a painter,

but my favorite is a photograph.
Do me the favor to burn this if you love me and believe me.

NOTES & ACKNOWLEDGEMENTS

NOTES

"Among Us" The words "release us from one war only to tie us to another and another" is taken from the article "Why the Dark Secrets of the First Gulf War Are Still Haunting Us" by Nora Eisenberg, AlterNet, February 27, 2009.

"Ballad of Winston Salem" was written for the "Carolina Circuit Writer" project for a performance at Winston-Salem Delta Fine Arts in response to the exoneration of Darryl Hunt who served 19 and a half years in prison, after being wrongfully convicted of the rape and murder of a 24-year-old white newspaper copy editor, Deborah Sykes.

"Before Dawn," "Lateral Wing," "Mecklenburg Evening," and "Ode to Romie" These poems were written for Romare Bearden (1911–1988) who was born in Charlotte. His family moved to New York City, but he always delved into his childhood memories throughout his lifetime for his artwork. He once said, "You have to go back to where you started to gain insights."

"Bird / Dream Conductor" was written from quotes and performance notes during Julie Patton's residency with the "Carolina Circuit Writer" project at the Afro-American Cultural Center in Charlotte.

"Cristo Redentor War Sonnets" were written in reply to a (Soma)tic Poetry Exercise by CA Conrad involving Donald Byrd's composition, "Cristo Redentor":

Dear Tony & Lee Ann,

I'm asking a handful of poets and others I know and respect to consider participating in this. Starting on December 22nd, at midnight, until December 26th at noon, I will be spending that 108 hours in seclusion working on a new (Soma)tic Poetry Exercise.

This one involves listening to the song "CRISTO REDEN-TOR" on a nonstop loop for the 108 hours. There are many other, more intricate details involved, but that's the gist of it,

TO GET INSIDE the walls of this powerful, amazing song. You can hear it here:
http://www.youtube.com/watch?v=w2KvM2T40RQ

What I'm asking is that you consider sending me an email between midnight 12/22 and noon 12/26 specifically talking to me LIKE YOU'RE GIVING A SPEECH about the escalation of war: 30,000 troops.

I do NOT believe in appropriation of text in this way of Postmodern theft, in other words whatever I use from what you write will be credited to you. I would NEVER use your words and make you anonymous, I loathe that very common practice of today.

If you choose to participate please write in the subject line WAR MESSAGE!

Thank you, now I'm going to go enjoy the snow,
Conrad,   12/19/09

"Ode to Uncle Billy" The first three lines are by Lorine Niedecker.

"333-2451 Susie Asado Breakdown" Written in a workshop led by Joan Retallack for the Institute for Writing & Thinking at Bard College, dedicated to Erica Hunt who said, "You sound like a Southern Gertrude Stein" and did some work down in Charlotte herself. Here, Stein's poem, "Susie Asado" breaks down through the methodical application of my parents' North Carolina phone number.

"Double Crown for Charlotte" Sources include: Print and visual resources found at The Robinson-Spangler Room of the Charlotte Mecklenburg Library; "The Blurred Racial Lines of Famous Families," *Frontline*, researched and written by Mario de Valdes y Cocom; *The Children's Miscellany: Useless Information That's Essential to Know; Court and Private Life in the Time of Queen Charlotte: being the journals of Mrs. Papendiek, assistant keeper of the wardrobe and reader to Her Majesty*; the 1994 film The *Madness of King George*, adapted by Alan Bennett from his play, *The Madness of George III; Queen Charlotte, 1744–1818: A Bilingual Exhibit* at the University of Virginia which includes on-line reproductions of Charlotte's own letters, as well as accounts by writers in her circles such as Horace Walpole, Fanny

Burney, and Mrs. Delany, as well a a letter from an eight-year-old Mozart's dedicating his Opus 3 to the Queen; *Queen Charlotte* by Olwen Hedley; various portraits including Sir Allan Ramsay's 1761 *Coronation Portrait of Queen Charlotte* and Ken Aptekar's 2010 six panel painting *Charlotte's Charlotte*, commissioned for the 250th anniversary of her coronation, both on permanent exhibit at the Mint Museum of Art in Charlotte; *Unexplained Presence* by Tisa Bryant (Leon Works).

> *O sing for that which*
> *is ordinary goes down to Orcus*
> *unsung*

are the last words of Schiller's *Nänie* set by Brahms.

ACKNOWLEDGEMENTS

Critical Quarterly
(guest editors: Stephen Boyer, William Scott)

Fence
(Rebecca Wolff, Caroline Crumpacker et al)

Fort Necessity
(editorial collective: Cynthia Nelson, Maggie Nelson, Lily Mazzarella, Jennie Portnof)

No, Dear
(Montana Ray + Emily Brandt + Alex Cuff)

Selected Essays About a Bibliography by Tan Lin

The Occupy Wall Street Poetry Anthology
(editorial collective)

Thanks to the librarians at the Robinson-Spangler Carolina Room at the Charlotte Mecklenburg Public Library and to my long lost neighbor, Sparky for telling me about Shuffletown. Thanks to the Gourd Lady. Thanks to Price's Chicken Coop for frying in peanut oil. Thank you to Kirsten Mullen and Julie Patton for including me in the Carolina Circuit Writers project. Thanks to Pete Crow, Susan Mead, Cece Conway and colleagues at the National Endowment for the Humanities' "Regional Study and the Liberal Arts: An Appalachian Exemplar" at Ferrum College. Thank you to the Howard Foundation for a poetry fellowship. Thank yous to my husband, Tony Torn for lessons in editorial trance and to my typo-feline, Miranda Torn, she who pounces on all typos. Thank you to all my family: gifted, elected, and extended, for so much love and support.

ALSO BY LEE ANN BROWN

Polyverse
The Sleep That Changed Everything
Bagatelles for Cornell (with Karen Randall)
In the Laurels, Caught

The text of the book is typeset in 10-point Minion.
The book was designed by Lesley Landis Designs.